11/10

Hanukkah

by **Trudi Strain Trueit**

Reading Consultant: Nanci R. Vargus, Ed.D.

Marshall Cavendish
Benchmark
New York

Picture Words

 candle

 candles

 chocolate coins

 doughnuts

dreidel

 gifts

 latkes

 menorah

We light the 🕎
on the eight nights
of Hanukkah.

We light one | for
each night.

We light 🕯️ and sing.

We light and make .

We light ▮▮▮ and

eat 🍩.

We light ███ and
play 🔯.

We light and
give .

We light and open .

The 🕎 is lit.
Happy Hanukkah!

Words to Know

dreidel (DRAY-duhl)
   a four-sided top used to play a
   Hanukkah game

Hanukkah (HAH-nuh-kah)
   the eight-day Jewish festival
   of lights

latkes (LAHT-kees)
   potato pancakes

menorah (meh-NOR-uh)
   a Hanukkah candleholder

Find Out More

Books

dePaola, Tomie. *My First Chanukah*. New York: Grosset & Dunlap, 2008.

Dice, Elizabeth A. *Christmas and Hanukkah*. New York: Chelsea House, 2009.

Sievert, Terri. *Hanukkah: Jewish Festival of Lights*. Mankato, MN: Capstone Press, 2006.

Websites

Chabad.org: Chanukah
www.chabad.org/holidays/chanukah/default_cdo/jewish/Hanukkah.htm

The History Channel: The History of Hanukkah
www.history.com/content/hanukkah/

About the Author

Trudi Strain Trueit is the author of more than fifty fiction and nonfiction books for children. *Kwanzaa, Christmas,* and *Thanksgiving* are among her titles for the Benchmark Rebus Holiday Fun series. Visit her website at **www.truditrueit.com**.

About the Reading Consultant

Nanci R. Vargus, Ed.D., wants all children to enjoy reading. She used to teach first grade. Now she works at the University of Indianapolis. Nanci helps young people become teachers. Her grandson Oliver celebrates Hanukkah in Montreal, Canada.

Copyright © 2011 Marshall Cavendish Corporation

Published by Marshall Cavendish Benchmark
An imprint of Marshall Cavendish Corporation

Other Marshall Cavendish Offices:
Marshall Cavendish International (Asia) Private Limited, 1 New Industrial Road, Singapore 536196 • Marshall Cavendish International (Thailand) Co Ltd. 253 Asoke, 12th Flr, Sukhumvit 21 Road, Klongtoey Nua, Wattana, Bangkok 10110, Thailand • Marshall Cavendish (Malaysia) Sdn Bhd, Times Subang, Lot 46, Subang Hi-Tech Industrial Park, Batu Tiga, 40000 Shah Alam, Selangor Darul Ehsan, Malaysia

Marshall Cavendish is a trademark of Times Publishing Limited

All websites were available and accurate when this book was sent to press.

Library of Congress Cataloging-In-Publication Data
Trueit, Trudi Strain.
Hanukkah / Trudi Strain Trueit.
       p. cm. — (Benchmark rebus. Holiday fun)
Includes bibliographical references.
Summary: "A simple introduction to Hanukkah using rebuses"—Provided by publisher.
ISBN 978-0-7614-4884-6
1. Hanukkah—Juvenile literature. 2. Rebuses—Juvenile literature. I. Title.
BM695.H3T744 2009
296.4'35—dc22
2009019068

Editor: Christina Gardeski
Publisher: Michelle Bisson
Art Director: Anahid Hamparian
Series Designer: Virginia Pope

Photo research by Connie Gardner
Cover photo by Brand X Pictures/*Art Life Images*

The photographs in this book are used by permission and through the courtesy of:
Corbis: p. 5 Richard Hutchings; p. 7 Ted Horowitz. *Getty Images:* p. 2 Steve Cole, candles; Photographers Choice, chocolate coins; Food collection, doughnuts; p. 3 Thomas Northcut, dreidel, menorah; C Squared Studios, gifts; Andy Crawford, latkes; p. 9 Sean Gallup; p. 17 Tom Grill; p. 21 Rob Meinychuk. *PhotoEdit:* p. 11 Bill Aron. *Alamy:* p. 13 Cathy Raff. *Art Life Images:* pp. 15, 19 Brand X.

Printed in Malaysia (T)
1 3 5 6 4 2